LAUREN SANCHEZ

THE UNTOLD STORY OF THE EXTRAORDINARY LIFE OF LAUREN SANCHEZ

Her Journey as a TV Personality, Hollywood Star, and an Entrepreneur.

Alex Grant

Copyright © 2023
All rights reserved

Table of Contents

Introduction

Chapter 1: A Journey Begins

Chapter 2: On Set and Ready for Action!

Chapter 3: The On-Air Personality

Chapter 4: Personal Life

Epilogue: A Legacy of Inspiration

Introduction

In the dazzling realm of fame and fortune, few individuals have captured the world's attention quite like Lauren Sanchez. From her captivating presence on television screens to her remarkable foray into the glitz and glamor of Hollywood, her journey has been nothing short of extraordinary. But behind the flashing lights and glossy façade lies a story waiting to be unveiled—a story of resilience, determination, and an unwavering spirit.

"The Untold Story of the Extraordinary Life of Lauren Sanchez" delves deep into the remarkable odyssey of a woman who has defied the odds and blazed her own trail. From her humble beginnings to becoming a prominent TV personality, Hollywood star, and entrepreneur, Sanchez's life is a testament to the power of ambition and the pursuit of dreams.

Join us as we embark on a captivating journey through the highs and lows, triumphs and tribulations that have shaped Lauren Sanchez's life. From her early days as a young dreamer with a vision, to her meteoric rise in the world of broadcasting, this book unveils the secrets and untold anecdotes that have shaped her extraordinary career.

Discover the challenges she faced, the risks she took, and the invaluable lessons she learned along the way. With each turn of the page, you will witness the indomitable spirit of a woman who fearlessly carved her own path, breaking barriers and redefining success on her own terms.

Through exclusive interviews, behind-the-scenes stories, and a rich tapestry of personal experiences, "The Untold Story of the Extraordinary Life of Lauren Sanchez" paints a vivid portrait of a true icon. It is a tale of determination, passion, and unwavering dedication—a story that will inspire and captivate readers from all walks of life.

Prepare to be enthralled as we peel back the layers and delve into the depths of a life lived in the spotlight. This is more than just a biography; it is an exploration of the human spirit and the pursuit of greatness. Get ready to experience the extraordinary as we uncover the untold story of Lauren Sanchez—a woman who has left an indelible mark on the world and continues to shine brightly in the realms of television, Hollywood, and entrepreneurship.

Chapter 1
A Journey Begins

Lauren Wendy Sánchez, born in Albuquerque, New Mexico, December 19, 1969, comes from a family of Mexican-American heritage, with parents who are second-generation immigrants.

From an early age, it was clear that Lauren possessed a natural spark and charisma that would set her on a path towards greatness.

Growing up in a close-knit family, Lauren was encouraged to dream big and reach for the stars. Her parents recognized her unique talents and nurtured her passions, allowing her to explore various creative outlets. From singing and dancing to performing in school plays, Lauren's natural talent for entertaining was evident to all who knew her.

As Lauren entered her teenage years, her aspirations began to take shape. Inspired by the glamor of television and the silver screen, she set her sights on a career in the entertainment industry. Determined to turn her dreams into reality, she immersed herself in the world of performing arts, honing her skills and learning the ins and outs of the industry.

In the early 1990s, during her educational years, Sánchez enrolled at El Camino College in Torrance, California, where she actively contributed to the school newspaper as a writer.

Her talent for journalism and her natural ability to connect with people propelled her forward. Lauren's articles not only informed but also inspired, shedding light on topics that were close to her heart. Whether it was showcasing the achievements of her fellow students or delving into thought-provoking social issues, she demonstrated an innate ability to capture the essence of a story and bring it to life.

The school newspaper became a launchpad for Lauren's aspirations, allowing her to refine her writing skills and nurture her innate curiosity about the world. It was during those formative years that she realized the power of media to inform, entertain, and inspire change. With each article she penned, her dreams grew bolder, and her determination to make an impact in the world of television deepened.

Little did she know that the path she embarked upon in those early days would shape her future in remarkable ways. As she penned her final article for the school newspaper, a new chapter in Lauren Sanchez's life was about to unfold—one filled with bright lights, captivating stories, and a journey that would take her from small-town dreams to the grand stages of Hollywood and beyond.

Chapter 2
On Set and Ready for Action!

As Lauren Sanchez bid farewell to her college years, she stood at the threshold of the unknown, ready to embrace the exhilarating world of television. Armed with ambition and an unwavering belief in her abilities, she set her sights on the bustling city of Los Angeles, where dreams were crafted and destinies were realized.

The vibrant energy of the entertainment industry welcomed Lauren with open arms. She dove headfirst into auditions, casting calls, and networking events, determined to carve a place for herself in the competitive world of television. It wasn't long before her natural charisma and magnetic presence caught the attention of industry insiders.

With her infectious smile and an undeniable on-screen charm, Lauren soon found herself making appearances on various television programs.

From hosting game shows to delivering captivating interviews, she effortlessly captivated audiences with her authentic and engaging persona. Her ability to connect with people on a profound level set her apart, leaving a lasting impression wherever she went.

But Lauren's journey was not without its challenges. Behind the glitz and glamour of the television industry lay countless auditions, rejections, and moments of self-doubt. Yet, through it all, she remained resilient, fueled by a burning passion to share stories that mattered and to leave a lasting impact on those who tuned in.

Her perseverance paid off as she secured a coveted position as a TV personality on a popular morning show. The stage was set for Lauren to shine, and she embraced the opportunity with unwavering enthusiasm. Week after week, she graced the screens of millions of viewers, delivering the news with a captivating blend of warmth, professionalism, and authenticity.

But Lauren's ambitions didn't stop at television. Her entrepreneurial spirit beckoned her to explore new horizons and create opportunities beyond the confines of a single platform. She ventured into producing, working behind the scenes to bring captivating stories to life. Her keen eye for talent and her ability to spot compelling narratives set her productions apart, garnering critical acclaim and expanding her influence in the industry.

As she navigated the ever-evolving landscape of the entertainment world, Lauren Sanchez became a force to be reckoned with—a trailblazer who fearlessly pushed boundaries and shattered glass ceilings. Her passion for storytelling and her dedication to her craft propelled her forward, earning her the respect and admiration of her peers.

Chapter 2 marked a turning point in Lauren's journey—a chapter filled with pivotal moments, exciting opportunities, and the unwavering determination to leave an indelible mark on the world of television. With each step she took, she moved closer to realizing her dreams and embracing the extraordinary life that awaited her.

Chapter 3
The On-Air Personality

Lauren Wendy Sánchez's career kickstarted as a desk assistant at KCOP-TV in Los Angeles. She then went on to hold various positions, including anchor and reporter at KTVK-TV in Phoenix. Later, Sánchez joined the popular syndicated entertainment show Extra as a reporter. She further expanded her portfolio by becoming an anchor and correspondent for the sports magazine Going Deep on Fox Sports Net, earning an Emmy nomination. Additionally, Sánchez served as an anchor for Fox Sports News Primetime and an entertainment reporter for FSN's Best Damn Sports Show Period.

In 1999, Sánchez returned to KCOP-TV, where she anchored UPN News 13 and received an Emmy Award. She also took on the role of an entertainment reporter for KTTV's 10pm news. Sánchez gained recognition as a contestant on season 2 of The View's nationwide hosting competition in 2000, ultimately securing the runner-up position. In 2005, she became the original host of the immensely popular dancing competition, So You Think You Can Dance, on FOX. After one season, she left the show to focus on motherhood.

In 2009, Sánchez made her way back to Extra as the weekend anchor and special correspondent. She continues to make appearances on shows like Good Day LA and remains active in the television industry. Sánchez's beauty and talent have been acknowledged by People magazine, featuring her in their "50 Most Beautiful" issue in 2010, and Us Weekly, including her in their "Hot Bodies" issue.

Lauren Wendy Sánchez achieved widespread recognition as an esteemed entertainment reporter and news anchor. Throughout her career, she has made notable appearances as a guest host on The View, served as a co-host on Good Day LA at KTTV Fox 11, anchored the Fox 11 News at Ten, and held the positions of anchor and special correspondent on Extra.

Sánchez's expertise and insights have also been sought after on prominent shows such as Larry King Live, The Joy Behar Show, and Showbiz Tonight, where she has regularly contributed her expertise and commentary.

Chapter 4
Personal Life

Entrepreneurial Spirit

In 2016, Lauren Wendy Sánchez established Black Ops Aviation, breaking barriers as the first female owner of an aerial film and production company. Presently, her primary focus revolves around engaging in film and television ventures that leverage her expertise as a licensed pilot of airplanes and helicopters.

Looking ahead, Sánchez envisions embarking on an extraordinary journey to space in early 2024. With a crew comprising solely of women, she anticipates boarding a New Shepard spacecraft for this groundbreaking mission.

In June 2016, Lauren Wendy Sánchez obtained her helicopter pilot's license, marking a significant milestone in her aviation journey. Subsequently, she founded Black Ops Aviation, an innovative aerial film and production company dedicated to capturing stunning visuals from the skies.

According to Page Six, the pilot was also enlisted to capture aerial shots for Blue Origin, a company owned by Bezos.

Additionally, she recently served as an aerial producer for Catherine Hardwicke's 2019 action/thriller film, Miss Bala, featuring Gina Rodriguez.

Currently, Sánchez directs her attention towards film and television endeavors that enable her to utilize her expertise as a licensed pilot of both airplanes and helicopters.

Taking on the role of vice chair, Sanchez is actively involved in the Bezos Earth Fund, an initiative established by Bezos himself. The primary focus of the fund is to address climate change and contribute to the preservation of the environment.

Family
Lauren Sanchez has three kids from her past

marriages and relationships.

From her previous relationship with former NFL tight end Tony Gonzalez, Sánchez welcomed her son, Nikko, in 2001. In August 2005, she entered into marriage with Patrick Whitesell, a Hollywood agent and co-founder of the Endeavor talent agency. Together with Whitesell, Sánchez has two children: a son named Evan, born in 2006, and a daughter named Ella, born in 2008.

Relationships & Marriages

On May 22, 2023, after a public relationship of four years, Bezos popped the question and proposed to Sánchez.

In 2019, romantic speculations surrounding Lauren Sánchez and Jeff Bezos surfaced.
However, the romantic relationship between Bezos and Sanchez began in 2018.

In 2018, Sánchez engaged in an extramarital affair with Jeff Bezos, the businessman and founder of Amazon, despite both individuals being married at the time. This affair ultimately resulted in Bezos divorcing his wife of 25 years, MacKenzie, with whom he had co-founded Amazon. Likewise, Sánchez's relationship with Bezos led to the dissolution of her marriage to Patrick Whitesell.

During the initial phase of their relationship, Sánchez, the former co-host of Good Day LA, was simultaneously going through a divorce from her husband of 13 years, Patrick Whitesell, who is renowned as one of Hollywood's most influential agents.

Lauren Sanchez and Patrick Whitesell got married in August 2005. Prior to the marriage to Whitesell, she had a relationship with NFL star Tony Gonzalez. Her relationship with Gonzalez ended in 2001 after the birth of their son.

Epilogue

A Legacy of Inspiration

Lauren Sanchez's extraordinary journey as a TV personality, Hollywood star, and entrepreneur has been one of immense passion, resilience, and trailblazing spirit.

Lauren Sanchez's story serves as a testament to the power of ambition and determination. From her humble beginnings as a journalist to her rise to prominence in the entertainment industry, she has constantly defied expectations and shattered glass ceilings. Her unwavering belief in herself and her abilities has inspired countless individuals to pursue their dreams fearlessly.

Throughout her career, Lauren has exemplified versatility and adaptability. Her ability to seamlessly transition between different roles and industries showcases her remarkable range of talents. Whether as a captivating TV personality, a celebrated actress, or an innovative entrepreneur, she has consistently demonstrated her ability to excel and make a lasting impact.

Beyond her professional achievements, Lauren's philanthropic endeavors have touched the lives of many. Her dedication to giving back to her community and supporting charitable causes has made a tangible difference in the lives of those in need. Her compassion and generosity serve as an inspiration for others to use their success and influence for the betterment of society.

Lauren's story is one of resilience in the face of adversity. Despite the challenges and setbacks she has encountered along the way, she has always persevered with unwavering determination. Her ability to navigate through tough times with grace and strength has set an example for others facing their own obstacles, reminding them that they too can overcome and achieve greatness.

As we close this book, we are left with a profound appreciation for the life and journey of

Lauren Sanchez. Her relentless pursuit of excellence, her commitment to making a difference, and her unwavering belief in the power of dreams have touched the lives of many. She has left an indelible legacy that will continue to inspire generations to come.

May the story of Lauren Sanchez serve as a beacon of hope and empowerment for all those who dare to dream and strive for greatness. Her remarkable journey reminds us that with passion, resilience, and a relentless pursuit of our goals, anything is possible.

Printed in Great Britain
by Amazon